FORGET MOTIVATION

EXTRAORDINARY EXAMPLE OF AN ORDINARY MAN

A journey through discipline, shadow work, and becoming unrecognizable

BY
RYAN HALLEY

Copyright © 2025 Ryan Halley

All rights reserved.
No part of this book may be reproduced or distributed in any form without written permission of the author.

AUTHOR

I was the overweight kid in special ed. I've worked as a personal trainer, real estate agent, and police officer—often all at once.

This isn't written from a beach. It's written on breaks between patrol calls and open house showings. I'm not a guru—I'm a guy still grinding. Still learning. Still becoming. I wrote this for the ones still in it too.

Instagram: @fckmotiv

fckmotiv@gmail.com

DEDICATION

To my parents—

Thank you for your constant support and for instilling in me the mindset to never quit.

Mom, your unconditional love has been my foundation.

Dad, you taught me that nothing is handed to you—you earn it through hard work and belief.

To my wife—

Thank you for believing in me, even when the road was uncertain. Your faith in me pushed me forward more than you know.

And to my children—

I hope this book becomes more than just words on a page.

I hope it's a pathway—a reminder that no matter where you start, with discipline, grit, and heart, you can build something extraordinary.

For the ones still grinding.

For the ones who get up tired,

who show up anyway,

who don't need applause to keep going.

This book is for you.

The unfinished.

The unfiltered.

The unstoppable.

Stay in the fight.

CONTENTS

Intro 6

    Chapter 01. The Labels We Wear 9

    Chapter 02. Chasing Validation 13

    Chapter 03. Reinvention & Rejection 18

    Chapter 04. The Motivation Lie 22

    Chapter 05. Shadow Work 26

    Chapter 06. Suffering Isn't the Enemy 31

    Chapter 07. The Law of Equivalent Exchange 35

    Chapter 08. Discipline Over Dopamine 39

    Chapter 09. Consistency Is King 43

    Chapter 10. Becoming Unstoppable 47

    Chapter 11. The Shadow Work 51

    Chapter 12. Building a Life That Feeds You 55

    Chapter 13. The Work Is the Way 59

    Chapter 14. Building While Bleeding 63

    Chapter 15. The Long Game 67

    Chapter 16. The Discipline Shift 71

Author's Note on Concepts Referenced 75

INTRO

This Isn't a Victory Lap I'm not writing this from a beach in Bali, or a high-rise overlooking Manhattan, or some polished studio with a personal brand team telling me how to posture success.

I'm writing this in between 12-hour patrol shifts and showing homes on my "days off," fighting to stay awake long enough to build a life I haven't quite figured out yet. I'm in it.

Still grinding. Still uncertain. Still dragging myself out of bed before the sun rises—not because I feel like it, but because I promised myself I would.

This isn't a "made it" story. This is a "making it" story. One of those middle chapters that no one likes to talk about. The messy middle. The chapter where you question everything—your worth, your path, your pace. The part where motivation is gone, clarity is a myth, and all you've got is grit and some half-healed wounds that still sting when touched.

If that's where you are—good. You're not behind. You're just in the fire. And fire doesn't destroy—it forges.

Why I'm Writing This. I was the overweight kid in special ed. The kid with a file that labeled me as "different." "Slow." "Special." And I carried that label into every room I walked into—classrooms, locker rooms, job interviews, adult relationships. I wasn't wearing it on my sleeve anymore, but it was stuck to my identity like a tattoo I never chose.

It planted a seed in me: you're not enough. And I watered that seed with everything I did for years—trying to prove I belonged. Trying to outwork the whispers in my head. Trying to outrun the version of me I couldn't stand.

So I chased validation. I crushed workouts. Became a personal trainer. Told myself if I could just fix my body, everything else would fall into place.

But it didn't. Then I pivoted—real estate. New hustle, new identity. That had to be the answer, right? But that path collapsed, too. So I found purpose. I became a cop. Thought maybe duty would quiet the inner chaos.

But even in uniform, I still felt like I was performing. Still aching for something deeper. Still looking for a feeling that never came. At some point, I realized I wasn't chasing success—I was running from myself.

What Changed

I stopped looking for the next fix. Stopped searching for the next title, the next hustle, the next hit of motivation. And I started facing the part of me I'd buried. The weak, scared, ashamed parts. The ones I hated.

Carl Jung called it the Shadow—the part of you that you reject, that lives in the dark corners of your psyche. I started studying it. Not like a scholar, but like a man desperate to make peace with himself. And slowly, painfully, I started dragging those parts into the light.

This book was born there—in the dark. Not after I found the answers, but while I was still asking the hard questions. Not after the success story, but during the uncomfortable, lonely, in-progress fight that most people skip over.

Who This Is For

This is for the ones in the suck. The ones who are tired of self-help books written from the top of the mountain by people who forgot what the valley feels like.

This is for the ones grinding through 60-hour weeks, fighting off imposter syndrome, doing the work without applause, and wondering if they're ever going to feel "whole." This is for you if you've ever felt behind. Like you're late to your own life. Like something's missing and you don't know what. I see you because I am you. Not the polished version—just the real one.

What You'll Find Here

This isn't a blueprint. There are no five-step formulas to your dream life. This is a story. A mirror. A punch in the gut and a hand on your shoulder.

You'll find:

- Stories from the grind, not the highlight reel.
- Principles, not platitudes.
- Shadow work, not surface-level hacks.
- Discipline, not dopamine.

You'll read about the days I wanted to quit. The careers I failed in. The identities I built and burned down. The quiet victories. The brutal realizations. The patterns I had to break. And through all of it, one message will echo over and over: Keep showing up. You Don't Have to Be Fixed to Move Forward.

Read that again.

You don't have to be healed, confident, or certain to take action. You just have to be willing to walk into the unknown while scared. You have to stop waiting for clarity and start moving with intention. You have to choose the hard road—not because it's heroic, but because it's real. And real is where change lives. Let's walk this path together. I'm not ahead of you. I'm just beside you, flashlight in hand, still figuring it out too. Let's go.

CHAPTER

01

THE LABELS WE WEAR

The Stories They Gave Us, and the Ones We Choose to Keep

I didn't ask for the label. Didn't raise my hand and volunteer to be "different." But that's what they called it. Special education. And when you're a kid, you don't know what that means—you just know you're not in the room with the "normal" kids. They said it gently, like it was a good thing. Like I was getting more "attention" or "support." But even at that age, I could feel what it really meant.

It meant: You don't belong here. It meant: You're not smart enough, fast enough, normal enough.

And maybe they shredded those files later. Maybe the system moved on. But I didn't. I carried that label like a scar that never quite faded. Not visible to others, but burning under my skin every time I walked into a room. When You're Labeled Early, You Learn to Hide

I started performing young. Not on a stage, but in life. Smiling when I was confused. Nodding like I understood. Acting like the words didn't sting when teachers or kids looked at me like I was a step behind. You learn to cover up. To adapt. To fake it. But underneath it all, the narrative gets written in permanent ink: You're not enough. You don't measure up. You're a problem to fix. It didn't matter how old I got—every new situation triggered that script. In the gym. In work. In relationships. Every failure didn't just hurt—it confirmed the story I believed about myself.

And that's the trap with early labels. They don't just define your past—they shape your future. Unless you rip them out by the root.

COMPENSATION BECOMES IDENTITY

So I overcompensated. I chased things that made me feel powerful—lifting, knowledge, success, even control.

I became a personal trainer not just to help people—but because I thought maybe, just maybe, if I could fix my body, I could finally outrun the label. Look the part. Act the part. Be the part. But all I really did was swap one mask for another.

From "slow" to "shredded." From "behind" to "high-achiever." From "insecure" to "alpha."

The problem wasn't the grind—it was what I was grinding for. Validation. Approval. Proof that I was good enough. But no amount of muscle can protect you from the stories you still believe in the dark. And no amount of hustle can silence the voice in your head whispering, you're still that kid.

Labels Aren't Truths—They're Traps. At some point, I realized something heavy: That label didn't define me—I just never challenged it. No one ever told me I could. I thought identity was fixed. Like some concrete foundation poured in childhood that you had to build on forever, no matter how crooked it was. But the truth is: You don't have to accept the first story you were given. That label you were handed? You didn't choose it. But you're choosing to carry it now. And if you can carry it, you can also put it down.

THE SHADOW STARTS HERE

Carl Jung said, "Until you make the unconscious conscious, it will direct your life and you will call it fate."

I didn't understand that at first. But over time, I realized that the parts of myself I rejected—my fear, my doubt, my past— weren't going away. They were just getting stronger in the dark. That "special ed" kid I buried? He started showing up in my self-doubt. In my perfectionism. In my self-sabotage. Not because he was broken—but because I was pretending he didn't exist. The Shadow isn't evil. It's not the villain. It's the wounded part of you asking to be seen.

And until you're willing to face it, you'll keep tripping over it in every area of your life.

YOU DON'T NEED TO PROVE YOU BELONG

I spent years trying to prove I was worthy of being in the room. But here's the truth I wish someone had told me sooner: You already belong. Not because you earned it. Not because you fixed yourself. But because you're human. You were never supposed to become someone else to be accepted.

You were supposed to become yourself. And sometimes, becoming yourself means revisiting the ugliest, most painful chapters of your life and rewriting the story from the inside out.

The Real Work Starts Here. This chapter isn't just about childhood. It's about whatever label you've carried —too dumb, too fat, too quiet, too loud, too broken, too late.

It's about questioning the narrative that shaped your identity. And deciding to write a new one—not with fake confidence, but with brutal honesty and relentless commitment. Because the past might explain you, but it doesn't define you. Not unless you let it.

REFLECTION PROMPT:

1. What label have you carried the longest?

2. Who gave it to you?

3. And what would your life look like if you stopped accepting it as truth?

CHAPTER 02

CHASING VALIDATION

*When Proving Yourself Becomes a
Full-Time Job*

Let's be honest—validation feels good. When people clap for you, compliment your progress, double-tap your transformation post, or tell you they're proud—you feel seen. You feel like maybe, finally, you're doing something right.

And when you've spent years believing you're not enough, those little bursts of approval feel like oxygen. That's where I lived for a long time. I wasn't chasing goals —I was chasing proof.

Proof that I wasn't broken.

Proof that I was worthy.

Proof that I could become the opposite of what that "special ed" label made me feel like I was.

THE GYM WAS MY ARMOR

For a while, the gym became my religion. Iron didn't judge me. Reps didn't call me slow. PRs didn't ask for a résumé. Every session was a ritual of self-redemption. I wasn't just building muscle—I was building a mask. I became a personal trainer because I wanted to help people, sure. But if I'm being brutally honest? I also became a trainer because I needed to be the guy who looked the part. The guy people respected on sight. The guy who walked into a room and didn't have to explain himself—because his body did the talking. And it worked—for a while. Clients came. Compliments rolled in. People told me I was inspiring. Disciplined. Alpha. But deep down, I knew what I was really doing: Trying to outrun the parts of myself I still hated.

THE TRAP OF LOOKING LIKE YOU HAVE IT ALL TOGETHER

In the self-help world, there's this addiction to looking like you're winning. You read the right books. You talk the talk. You stack your wins. You post the grind.

But at some point, the image starts to matter more than the identity. You confuse progress with performance. That's where I was.

I wasn't building a life—I was curating an image.

And eventually, that cracks. Because when the likes stop… when the attention fades…when motivation dies out… you're left with the same internal silence you started with. And if you never healed what's underneath, it hits harder than ever.

Realization: Progress Without Peace Is Just Panic in Disguise. I started to see that I wasn't chasing goals out of joy—I was running out of fear.

Fear of being average.

Fear of being invisible.

Fear of becoming that kid again—the one who was left behind.

And the thing about fear is… it never runs out of fuel. No matter how hard you work, fear will always find a new way to whisper, "It's not enough."

THE COST OF EXTERNAL VALIDATION

Let's talk about the real cost of chasing validation:

- You stop doing things because you love them. You do them because they get claps.
- You stop trusting your gut. You wait for permission to move.
- You can't sit in silence without wondering if you're falling behind.
- You burn out. Not because you're weak —but because the grind you're in isn't even yours.

When you chase validation, you become a slave to opinions. When they love you, you rise. When they go quiet, you collapse. It's not sustainable. And it sure as hell isn't fulfilling.

SO I BURNED OUT

The fitness career that once gave me life started to feel like a trap. My heart wasn't in it anymore. Not because I didn't care—but because I couldn't fake it. I hit that wall where the hustle didn't work.

I was showing up, doing the sessions, posting the content, but it all felt hollow. I wasn't fulfilled—I was performing. And eventually, the mask got too heavy. That's when I made the pivot into real estate. I thought maybe this would be the thing. New role. New opportunity. New identity. But I was making the same mistake again—chasing another form of external success, hoping it would fix an internal problem. It didn't.

WHEN THE FLAME OF MOTIVATION DIES

I used to be hooked on motivation. I'd watch the videos. Hype myself up. Post the quotes. But here's what no one tells you: Motivation dies. Every time. It burns bright at the start—but it doesn't last through the suck. It disappears when results are slow, when praise dries up, when you're left alone with your thoughts. And when motivation dies, what's left? If you don't have something deeper— some inner anchor— you crash. That's what happened to me. And in that crash, I started asking the real questions:

- Why am I doing this?
- Who am I trying to impress?
- What am I trying to prove?
- Who would I be if no one was watching?

That's when the real work began. Validation Isn't the Enemy—But It Can't Be the Fuel. Let me be clear: Validation isn't evil. We're human. We all want to feel seen. But if validation is your fuel—you'll stall every time the applause stops. Your fuel has to be something stronger. Something internal. Something that doesn't need claps to keep going. Discipline. Purpose. Peace. Self- respect. When you can find those things in silence—when you can keep showing up even when nobody sees you—that's when you know you're on the right path.

REFLECTION PROMPT:

1. Where in your life are you performing instead of living?
2. What would it look like to do the work—even if no one clapped?

CHAPTER 03

REINVENTION & REJECTION

Starting Over Isn't Weak—It's Necessary

There's this lie we're told: That once you pick a path, you have to stick with it. That changing careers, shifting passions, or starting over means you failed.

But what if it's the opposite?

What if reinvention isn't failure—it's evolution? I've reinvented myself more than once. Not because I'm indecisive. Not because I can't commit. But because I kept outgrowing versions of myself I once thought were permanent. And with every reinvention, I got rejected—by people, by systems, by my own expectations. But I also got refined.

The Trainer Who Fell Out of Love with Training. I became a personal trainer because I believed fitness could fix me. Fix my body. My confidence. My sense of worth. And for a while, it did. Training gave me structure. It gave me identity. It gave me control. But over time, I felt myself drifting. Not from the gym—but from the why behind it. I started feeling disconnected. Burned out. Uninspired. And when your heart isn't in something, your results will eventually reflect that.

I was afraid to admit it at first—because this was who I was. I was the trainer. The fit guy. The one people looked up to. To walk away from that meant letting go of an identity I'd worked so hard to build. But here's the truth most people won't tell you: When your identity becomes a prison, it's time to break out.

Jumping into Real Estate: Chasing the Next "Fix". So I pivoted. Real estate looked like the move. The freedom. The money. The challenge. It was appealing—especially coming off burnout from the fitness world.

But deep down, I wasn't running toward something—I was running from something. I thought success in this new field would erase the doubt I still carried. That if I sold enough, earned enough, posted enough wins—I'd finally feel "enough." But real estate didn't heal the internal gap. It just exposed it.

I struggled. Failed. Got humbled fast. No clients. No traction. No momentum. Just me—sitting in front of my laptop at night wondering if I had made the biggest mistake of my life. And yet… I wasn't broken. I was just being forced to confront something I had been avoiding: You can't out-hustle what you haven't healed.

Law Enforcement:

Searching for Purpose in the Uniform. After real estate, I joined the police force. Not because I wanted power—but because I wanted purpose. I thought maybe this would be the missing piece. Structure. Duty. Meaning. A job that mattered. And it did give me those things. But even then… the void wasn't filled. Even in the uniform, with a badge, with a title that demanded respect—I still felt like I was acting. Not because the job wasn't real. But because I still hadn't faced the internal war. Purpose can't be borrowed from a title. It has to come from within.

Reinvention Isn't Failure—It's a Feature of Growth Every time I changed careers, people asked: "Why can't you just stick with something?" But here's what they didn't understand: I wasn't quitting. I was transforming.

Reinvention isn't about flakiness—it's about refusing to stay where your soul is shrinking. It's not easy. You lose people. You lose stability. You lose your footing. But you gain something more important: Alignment. Each pivot brought me closer to who I actually am—not who I was trying to be.

REJECTION AS REDIRECTION

Rejection hurts. Whether it's from clients, bosses, opportunities, or your own inner critic. But over time, I've learned something powerful: Rejection isn't always the enemy. It's often the compass.

Every door that closed pushed me somewhere I was meant to go. Every person who doubted me taught me how to believe in myself. Every plan that fell apart revealed what wasn't truly for me. It doesn't feel good in the moment—but if you lean in, rejection becomes one of the best teachers.

LETTING GO OF OLD VERSIONS OF YOU

One of the hardest parts of reinvention is grieving the old you. Even when you know you've outgrown it, there's a part of you that clings to the familiar.

The identity you built.

The title you wore.

The praise you got.

But growth means killing your darlings — letting go of the comfortable illusions so you can make room for who you're becoming. And that hurts. But it's also the price of leveling up. This Isn't About Finding the "Right" Path—It's About Becoming the Right Person

What I've learned is this: There is no "perfect" path. No one road that leads to your best life. The path becomes right when you become right. When you stop chasing titles and start building character. When you stop looking for fixes and start building a foundation. When you stop performing and start aligning.

That's what this season of my life is about. Not the final destination. Not the shiny results. Just the daily grind of becoming the kind of man I don't need to escape from.

REFLECTION PROMPT:

1. Where in your life are you clinging to an identity that no longver fits?
2. What version of yourself do you need to let go of so you can evolve?

CHAPTER

04.

THE MOTIVATION LIE

*What You Do When You Don't
Feel Like It Is Who You Really Are*

I used to think motivation was the magic key. That if I could just stay motivated, I could do anything. So I chased it.

Motivational videos.

Podcasts.

Hype speeches.

Instagram quotes with lions and bold fonts screaming "RISE AND GRIND." It worked—for about 15 minutes. Then the same voice that used to say "You got this" started whispering, "What's the point?" That's the problem with motivation. It's a sugar high. A temporary kick in the ass that fades the moment real life hits. And if motivation is your fuel, you'll stall every single time the road gets rough.

The High of Starting—and the Crash That Follows Starting is sexy. That Day 1 energy? Addictive. New notebook. New workout plan. New side hustle. You feel unstoppable. Until it's not new anymore. Until the soreness sets in. Until the results are slower than the promises. Until no one's watching. That's when most people quit—not because they're weak, but because they were never taught the difference between motivation and discipline.

Motivation Asks "Do You Feel Like It?" Discipline Says "We're Doing It Anyway.

Motivation is emotional. It relies on your feelings And feelings? They change with sleep, stress, weather, hormones, and a million other things you can't control. Discipline doesn't ask for your permission. It doesn't care if you're tired, scared, anxious, or bored. It just shows up. I learned that the hard way.

When I was trying to rebuild my real estate momentum, I waited for the "spark." But the spark never came. And I realized—if I kept waiting for the perfect mood, I'd never get anything done. So

I stopped asking how I felt. I started asking: What's the next step? And can I take it—regardless of how I feel?

That shift changed everything. Consistency Isn't Sexy—But It's Sacred. No one claps when you make 10 cold calls and get hung up on 9 times. No one applauds when you show up to the gym on a rainy Tuesday with zero energy. No one sees the late nights you grind after a full shift at work. But those are the moments that build you.

Motivation loves the spotlight. Discipline thrives in the dark. And if you want real growth—lasting transformation—you need to fall in love with the boring stuff. The mundane. The unsexy. The daily actions that compound into momentum.

THE LAW OF DIMINISHING INTENT

There's a principle I learned that punched me in the chest:

The Law of Diminishing Intent. It says: The longer you wait to do something, the less likely you are to do it.

That means inspiration has an expiration date. Every time you get a good idea or feel a fire ignite—and you don't act—that fire shrinks. You tell yourself, "I'll start tomorrow," but tomorrow never has the same heat. The delay kills the drive. So now, when I feel inspired to do something— even a small step—I do it immediately. Not because I'm in the mood, but because I know the mood won't last. You don't need more motivation. You need more movement.

You're Not Lazy—You're Addicted to the Spark Let me be real: If you think you're lazy, you're probably not. You're just used to operating from emotion instead of intention. You've trained yourself to wait for fire before you move. But real growth? That comes from moving when there's no fire. Discipline is a muscle. And every time you show up without hype, you're strengthening it. Eventually, you stop needing motivation. Because momentum starts carrying you.

Show Up Anyway

Tired? Show up.

Uninspired? Show up.

Doubt creeping in? Show up.

No results yet? Show up.

That's the formula.

The goal isn't to feel good all the time —it's to build the kind of person who does the work anyway. Because if you only train when you feel like it... Only post when people are watching... Only chase your dream when you're in the mood... You'll live your whole life starting and stopping. Riding highs. Crashing in lows. Never getting anywhere. But if you make the decision to show up—regardless of mood, weather, or fear? You become dangerous. You become unstoppable.

REFLECTION PROMPT:

1. Where are you waiting to "feel ready" before you act?
2. What would your life look like if you stopped waiting—and just started?

CHAPTER 05.

SHADOW WORK

Facing the Parts You Want to Ignore

You ever feel like there's a version of you in the background—one that you're constantly trying to outrun? Not the polished version. Not the one with the goals and the habits and the morning routine.

I'm talking about the one that's insecure. Angry. Shameful. The part that sabotages you the moment things start going right. That's your Shadow. And until you face it, it'll run your life. What Is Shadow Work?

Shadow work is based on the psychology of Carl Jung. He said every person has a "shadow self"—the part of us made up of everything we deny, suppress, or reject.

Your shame.

Your rage.

Your jealousy.

Your insecurity.

Your self-sabotaging patterns.

All of it.

And guess what? Pretending that part of you doesn't exist doesn't make it go away. It makes it stronger. Because the Shadow doesn't disappear. It just hides—and influences you from the dark.

HOW I MET MY SHADOW

My Shadow showed up in every room I walked into, even when I looked successful. It was the voice that said, "You're still that slow kid from special ed." It was the part of me that needed people to validate me before I believed in myself. It was the anger I stuffed down anytime I felt overlooked or underestimated. It was the fear that I'd never be enough, no matter how many titles I earned. I spent years trying to cover it up —with muscle, with hustle, with status. But no matter how high I climbed, that internal weight kept pulling me back down. Until I finally stopped running.

The Mirror. You're Avoiding Shadow work starts with brutal honesty. It's about holding up a mirror—not to judge yourself, but to see yourself.

Here's what that looks like:

- Admit when you're jealous.
- Own when you're triggered—not blame others for it.
- Ask yourself why failure feels safer than success.
- Question the stories you tell yourself when you fall short
- Look at the patterns you keep repeating —and ask, "What part of me benefits from this?"

Most people avoid this kind of work. They'd rather stay distracted, blame their circumstances, or keep chasing new goals hoping it fixes the internal stuff. But nothing external will heal what's been buried inside. Not until you face it.

The Cost of Avoidance. When you avoid your Shadow, it shows up in sneaky ways:

- You self-sabotage the moment things go well.
- You ghost opportunities that scare you.
- You explode at small things because you're carrying big pain.
- You stay "busy" but avoid being alone with your thoughts.

Avoidance is easier short term—but it costs you long term peace, progress, and clarity. You can't outrun the parts of you you're unwilling to face.

How to Start Shadow. Work. You don't need a therapist to begin (though therapy helps). You need honesty, curiosity, and courage.

Here's how I started:

1. **Journaling Without Filters**

I'd write out thoughts I'd never say out loud. Rage. Jealousy. Shame. Insecurity. It was ugly—but it was real. And real is the first step to healing.

2. **Tracking Triggers**

Every time I overreacted to something, I paused and asked, "What's this really about?" Almost always, it wasn't about the person. It was about an old wound.

3. **Sitting in Silence**

No phone. No podcast. No stimulation. Just me and my mind. That's where the truth bubbles up. And at first—it's loud. But if you stay with it, the chaos starts to make sense.

4. **Owning My Story**

Instead of trying to rewrite my past, I started embracing it. I was the overweight kid. The kid who got labeled. The guy who felt behind. And all of that? It made me. It's not my weakness—it's my origin.

THE POWER OF INTEGRATION

Shadow work isn't about fixing yourself. It's about integrating all parts of you— so you're whole, not fractured. It's learning to say: "Yeah, I've got dark parts. But they don't control me anymore." Once you face your Shadow, you stop being afraid of it. And once you stop being afraid of it, you stop being afraid of yourself. And that's when you start moving with power.

Light Comes Through the Cracks Here's what I know now:

You don't grow just by adding more to your plate. You grow by digging into the why behind what you do. You grow by dragging the shame into the light. By naming the fear. By looking your patterns in the face and choosing differently. That's the real flex. Not just grinding harder—but healing deeper. Because when you stop hiding, you stop holding yourself back.

REFLECTION PROMPT:

1. What part of yourself have you been avoiding, denying, or judging?

2. What if facing that part is exactly what will set you free?

CHAPTER 06.

SUFFERING ISN'T THE ENEMY

It's the Training Ground for Who You're Becoming

We spend our whole lives trying to avoid pain. We numb it. Distract from it. Outwork it. Scroll past it.

We treat suffering like a detour—like if we were doing life "right," we wouldn't hurt so much. But I've learned something in the trenches: Suffering isn't the problem—it's the process. It's not a punishment. It's a proving ground. It forges what comfort never could. Pain Is a Teacher. No one likes pain. I'm not here to glorify it or tell you to seek it out for fun. But pain teaches you what ease never will.

- When you're broke, you learn resourcefulness.
- When you're rejected, you learn resilience.
- When you're alone, you learn to hear your own voice.
- When you're humbled, you learn who you really are.

Pain doesn't mean you're broken. It means you're in the fire where real things are formed. The Resistance Is the Rep. You know this from the gym: The growth comes from the struggle. The muscle breaks before it rebuilds stronger. It's the exact same with your mind. Your habits. Your identity. Every time you choose to sit in discomfort instead of escape it, you're repping something bigger than discipline —you're building identity

You're saying:

"I can suffer without quitting."

"I can feel pain without folding."

"I can be in the valley and still walk forward."

That kind of strength doesn't come from hype. It comes from the hurt.

Running From Pain Keeps You Stuck. Most people never grow because they run the second it hurts. They start a business— then quit when the sales aren't there. They commit to the gym—then stop when the soreness hits. They chase healing—until the inner work starts cutting too deep. The breakthrough is always on the other side of what you're avoiding. If you can learn to lean into discomfort—not chase it, but face it—you unlock a whole new level of power. Because suffering doesn't shrink you unless you let it.

"Why Me?" vs. "What's This Teaching Me?"

There was a point where I kept asking, "Why do I have to struggle this much?"

Why was I the kid with the label?

Why did I have to start over—again? Why did I never feel "there"?

But eventually, I started asking different questions:

- What is this moment building in me?
- What strength am I learning by not giving up?
- How will this pain serve someone else down the road?

That switch—from victim to student— changed everything. Because once you stop fighting the suffering and start working with it, it becomes fuel. Suffering Reveals the Real You. You don't know who you are when things are easy.

You find out when it all falls apart.

- When the deal dies.
- When the breakup blindsides you.
- When the numbers drop.
- When no one texts back.
- When you're dead tired, but the work still has to get done.

That's when you meet yourself. That's when your character either caves or climbs. And if you can suffer with integrity—if you can keep showing up when it doesn't make sense—you become dangerous in the best way. Because the person who doesn't need comfort to move? That person is unshakable.

The Gift in the Hurt. I wouldn't wish some of my lowest moments on anyone. But I also wouldn't trade them for anything. Because they gave me things success never did:

- Grit
- Clarity
- Empathy
- Fire
- Hunger
- Humility
- Discipline

Success didn't give me those. Suffering did. Don't Waste the Pain. Pain is inevitable. But transformation? That's optional. Most people waste the pain. They numb it. Hide it. Rush through it. But if you stay awake in the fire—if you keep your eyes open instead of shutting down—you walk out refined. Not just motivated. Not just smarter. But different. You walk out with depth. With perspective. With purpose. And the pain? It didn't break you. It built you.

REFLECTION PROMPT:

1. What pain are you currently facing—and what might it be building in you?

2. What if this season isn't the curse you think it is, but the construction zone for your next level?

CHAPTER 07.

THE LAW OF EQUIVALENT EXCHANGE

Everything Costs Something

There's a law I came across that wrecked my excuses and rewired my mindset. The Law of Equivalent Exchange. It comes from alchemy—and later, anime. But don't let that throw you off. The principle is deadly real:

"In order to gain something, you must give up something of equal value."

Want more success?

You have to give up comfort. Want a stronger body? You have to give up convenience. Want deep purpose and clarity? You have to give up distraction and denial. Everything costs something. If you're not paying the price, you're not making the progress.

You Already Know This

You know this in the gym. You don't just wish for strength—you trade your comfort for reps. You sacrifice time, sleep, soreness, food cravings. The exchange is clear. But when it comes to life? We forget this. We want success without risk. Growth without discomfort. Change without cost. That's not how anything real works. You don't get freedom without paying the price in sweat, time, or tears. You don't build discipline without saying no to easy. The exchange is always there. The question is: Are you willing to pay it? You Can't Have It All. Not at Once. Social media will lie to you. It'll sell you the illusion that you can "have it all" right now. The six-figure business. The shredded body. The healed inner child. The perfect relationship. The travel. The peace. The purpose. All at once.

But what it doesn't show is the trade-offs. You want to build a business? That might mean missing parties. You want to get fit? That means saying no to late-night DoorDash. You want to write a book? That's hours of staring at a screen while your friends are out. You can't plant ten seeds and harvest them all at once. You can have it all eventually—just not simultaneously. Life demands focus. It demands sacrifice. And if you're not choosing what to give up —you're probably giving up your future for your now.

The Invisible Cost of Staying the Same

You know what's wild? Even staying the same costs you something. It costs:

- Regret
- Confidence
- Time
- Missed opportunities
- Inner peace

So if you think not making a choice is "safe"? You're wrong. You're still trading— you're just not trading up. Every day you stay in your comfort zone, you're paying for it with your potential.

My Personal Exchange Rates. Here's what I've traded so far:

- I gave up sleeping in for momentum in my goals.
- I gave up validation for inner freedom.
- I gave up ease for identity.
- I gave up certainty for purpose.
- I gave up fitting in so I could finally stand up.

None of it was easy. But every single trade gave me something more valuable in return. It didn't come fast. It didn't come clean. But it came. And it'll come for you, too—if you stop avoiding the exchange.

How to Make Smarter Trades. You don't need to give up everything. But you do need to get clear on wha matters most.

Here's how:

1. **Define Your Target**

   What are you actually building? Be specific. Vague goals don't inspire commitment.

2. **Identify the Cost**

   Ask yourself: What is this going to demand from me? Time? Energy? Money? Attention? Sleep? Comfort?

3. **Choose to Pay It**

   Decide on purpose to make the trade. Don't drift into it—step into it.

4. **Audit Often**

Every week, ask: What am I sacrificing right now? Is it moving me toward my highest goal—or just draining me?

That level of awareness makes you dangerous. Because now you're not a victim of your circumstances—you're the one writing the terms of yourb transformation. What Are You Willing to Give Up? You say you want to change. You say you want more. You say you're hungry. Okay. So... what are you willing to trade for it? Because if your answer is "nothing," then your desire is just a wish. But if your answer is "whatever it takes"—then we're in business.

REFLECTION PROMPT:

1. What do you want most right now?
2. What's it going to cost you— and are you willing to pay that price?

CHAPTER 08.

DISCIPLINE OVER DOPAMINE

Becoming the Kind of Person Who Finishes

I used to be a dopamine junkie. The hype video. The perfect playlist. The motivational speaker screaming in my earbuds. The pump-up before the workout. The YouTube clips telling me I'm a lion, a beast, a savage. That stuff feels like fuel. But it burns out fast. Because dopamine is quick. It's light. It's surface. Discipline is deep. It's what's still standing when the motivation wears off.

Motivation Is a Spark—Discipline Is a Fire Let me put it this way:

Motivation is showing up when you feel like it. Discipline is showing up even when you don't. Motivation is emotion. Discipline is identity. If you're building your life on motivation, you're building on sand. You're depending on feelings to do the heavy lifting. But feelings are unreliable. They change with sleep, food, stress, likes, weather, whatever. Discipline doesn't ask how you feel. It asks, "What's the job?" And then it gets to work. Discipline Is a Skill, Not a Trait. You weren't "born lazy." You just trained inconsistency. Good news? You can train discipline the same way.

- Start small.
- Show up daily.
- Keep promises to yourself.
- Forgive the misses, but don't excuse them.
- Repeat.

Discipline isn't about being perfect. It's about being consistent enough to gain real traction. You won't feel like it most days. That's not a problem—it's part of the process.

Stop Waiting to Feel Ready This was a game changer for me: You don't need to feel like doing something in order to do it. Re-read that. We waste years waiting to feel "ready." To feel "fired up." To feel "inspired." But what if you just acted anyway? What if you trained your nervous system to show up regardless of emotion? That's discipline. And that's freedom. Because once you stop needing a vibe, you stop being a slave to your emotions. You become reliable. And reliable people finish what they start.

EMOTION DOESN'T EQUAL ACTION

This one hurt: Just because you felt inspired doesn't mean you did something. You can spend hours in your head, visualizing success. You can watch the reels, read the books, listen to the podcasts. But if you're not acting—you're high on dopamine, not building discipline.

Dopamine gives you the illusion of progress. Discipline is the only thing that produces real results. Practical Ways to Build Discipline. You don't need to be a machine. You need a system. Here's what works for me:

1. **Anchor Habits**

   Pick 1–2 non-negotiable. Small, daily. (Example: 10 minutes of reading, 3 minutes of movement.) Don't break the chain.

2. **Plan When You're Clear**

   Set your schedule the day before, not in the moment. Emotional brains make emotional decisions. Clear minds make strategic moves.

3. **Use the 5-Minute Rule**

   Start the task—even if it's just for 5 minutes. Momentum usually kicks in once you begin.

4. **Track Wins, Not Just Effort**

   Track what got done, not just what you meant to do. Don't reward intention— reward execution.

5. **Audit Your Inputs**

   Cut down on dopamine-heavy stuff that drains your drive. Scrolling, bingeing, over-consuming = discipline killers.

Discipline Makes You Dangerous When you become the person who keeps showing up:

- Even when it sucks
- Even when no one's watching
- Even when it's boring
- Even when there's no applause

You separate yourself. You stop needing permission. You stop needing hype. You stop needing dopamine to do the damn work. That's when the shift happens. You stop being the guy trying to get it —and start becoming the guy who is it.

REFLECTION PROMPT:

1. Where are you still relying on motivation to get moving?
2. What would it look like to build a version of you that shows up no matter what?

CHAPTER
09.

CONSISTENCY IS KING
Building Momentum in the Mud

Everybody loves the idea of consistency. Until they realize what it actually requires:

- Doing the thing when it's boring.
- Showing up when it's inconvenient.
- Taking action when it doesn't feel like it's working.

Consistency isn't sexy. It's not loud. It's not viral. But it's the most underrated superpower of anyone trying to become something more. Start. Keep Going. Don't Stop. That's it. That's the whole game. You don't need the perfect plan. You don't need a breakthrough moment. You don't need to "figure it all out" before you move. You need to start, Then keep going, And don't stop.

The ones who win aren't the smartest— they're the ones who refuse to quit when it gets quiet.

Your Results Are Lagging Indicators. Consistency will fool you. You'll put in work and… nothing. No progress. No applause. No payoff. It'll feel like you're pushing a boulder uphill. Day after day. Effort in. Silence out. But what's really happening? You're stacking invisible wins. Your actions today are seeds. You won't see the fruit until later— sometimes way later. Most people quit before the growth breaks the surface. They stop digging three feet from gold. They burn the field before the harvest. Don't be most people.

Momentum Lives in the Mundane. You want momentum? It doesn't come from "big moves." It comes from boring moves done with ruthless consistency.

- Hitting your macros.
- Making the follow-up calls.
- Sending the emails.
- Writing the pages.

- Stretching. Reading. Showing up.

No moment feels magical. But over time, the mundane becomes momentum. One brick at a time, the wall is built. One step at a time, the mountain is climbed.

Success Loves Boring People. You know who wins?

- The guy who makes the same calls every day.
- The woman who packs her lunch every week.
- The kid who reads 10 pages every night.
- The cop who shows up to every shift, early.
- The real estate agent who keeps marketing even when no one's biting.

Not because they're flashy. Because they're relentless. They've made peace with repetition. They've learned to love the work. They're not addicted to variety— they're addicted to growth.

HOW TO STAY CONSISTENT WHEN IT SUCKS

Let's be real—there will be days when consistency feels pointless. Here's how I keep moving through the mud:

1. **Micro-Wins**

Shrink the goal. Can't do 60 minutes at the gym? Do 15. Can't write 1,000 words? Write 100. Move the needle—even if it's barely noticeable.

2. **Stack Identity**

Every action is a vote for the kind of person you're becoming. Even when the results are missing, remind yourself: "This is who I am now."

3. **Track the Chain**

Use a habit tracker. Don't break the streak. The visual proof of progress keeps you mentally in the game.

4. **Revisit Your Why**

Don't just remember what you're doing— remember why. Purpose > pressure. When you reconnect with the deeper reason, you refuel.

5. **Kill Perfection**

Consistency doesn't mean flawless. It means frequent. Show up messy. Show up tired. But show up.

Fall in Love With Reps, Not Results. If you're obsessed with outcomes, you'll burn out. If you fall in love with reps, you'll outlast everyone. The world belongs to people who are consistent in silence. While others chase sparks, you build fires. While they jump ship, you're still rowing. That's how you become unshakable— not by hype, but by habit.

REFLECTION PROMPT:

1. What's one thing you know you need to do consistently—no matter how boring, slow, or unrewarded it feels right now?

CHAPTER
10.

BECOMING UNSTOPPABLE
Building a Standard That Doesn't Budge

Everyone wants to feel unstoppable. But most people are just temporarily motivated. Not truly built. They show up when it's convenient. They work hard when it feels good. They commit as long as the results show up quickly.

But becoming unstoppable? That's different. That's about creating a standard so locked in, it doesn't matter what's happening around you—because you already decided who you are within you.

Motivation Is a Visitor. Standards Are Home. Motivation is a guest—it shows up when it wants to, stays for a little while, then bounces. Your standard is what's left when motivation leaves. Your standard is what you expect from yourself even on your worst day. It's what you do when you're:

- Exhausted
- Stressed
- Discouraged
- Lonely
- Tempted to quit

Most people let their circumstances set the bar. But the ones who become unstoppable—they are the bar. This Isn't About Being Perfect— It's About Being Solid. Your standard doesn't mean you never mess up. It means when you fall off, you don't stay off. It means when it's hard, you still show up. When it's slow, you still believe. When it's lonely, you still lead yourself. You stop negotiating with excuses. You stop lowering the bar to meet your feelings—and start raising your actions to match your vision. Stop Saying "I'll Try" Trying is a trap. It leaves back doors open. It gives you permission to tap out the second it's uncomfortable. Want to become unstoppable? Close the doors. Burn the plan B. Start saying:

- "This gets done."
- "This is who I am now."

- "There is no version of me that doesn't follow through."

That's not arrogance. That's alignment. How to Build an Unshakable Standard. Let's break it down:

1. **Decide Who You Are**

    Write it out. Be specific. "I'm the type of person who…"
    Example: "I'm the type of person who trains daily, owns my word, and keeps moving forward—no matter the season."

2. **Audit the Gaps**

    Where are you not living up to that identity? No shame—just clarity. Close the gap one choice at a time.

3. **Create Rituals, Not Routines**

    Routines are tasks. Rituals have meaning. When you ritualize your habits, you build emotional buy-in and spiritual grit.

4. **Own Your Environment**

    If your surroundings weaken your standard —change them. People. Screens. Spaces. Noise. Audit what's draining your edge.

5. **Lead Yourself First**

    Stop waiting for accountability. Be your own leader. Champions don't wait to be told what to do—they set the tone.

Be the Storm. Everyone says they want peace. But most people are just trying to avoid chaos. Being unstoppable means something else: You're not afraid of the storm— You become it. When life hits hard, you don't scatter. You center. You lock in. You advance. That's what happens when your standard is higher than your circumstances.

From Pressure to Power. People will wonder how you keep showing up. How you keep building. Keep training. Keep grinding. Keep believing. They won't see your spreadsheet. They won't see the early mornings or the cold showers or the 9 PM real estate calls after your 12-hour patrol shift. They'll only see what consistency built. And by then, you won't need to explain it. Because you won't just do unstoppable things— You'll be an unstoppable person.

REFLECTION PROMPT:

1. What's your current standard?
2. What would your life look like if you raised it —even just 10%— this week?

CHAPTER

11.

THE SHADOW WORK

Facing the Parts of You You've Tried to Bury

There's a part of you you don't post. A part of you you avoid, deny, hide, or numb. That's your Shadow.

Carl Jung put it this way: "Until you make the unconscious conscious, it will direct your life and you will call it fate." Read that again. Slowly. The pain you don't face? The fear you won't name? The shame you keep stuffing down? That's what's running your life.

Not your to-do list.

Not your vision board.

Not your 5 a.m. wake-up time.

The Shadow runs deeper. What Is the Shadow? The Shadow is every part of you you've rejected. It's the insecurity. The envy. The anger. The laziness. The ego. The inner critic. The scared little kid who still feels not good enough. You buried these parts so you could be liked, accepted, or "functioning." But buried doesn't mean gone. What you suppress turns into sabotage.

Mine Looked Like This:

- Overworking to avoid stillness
- Being "productive" to avoid feeling unworthy
- Seeking attention so I didn't feel invisible
- Obsessing over being disciplined so I didn't have to face feeling broken
- Judging others to protect my own fragile ego

I wore the mask of motivation. But underneath was fear—fear of being found out. Fear of not being enough. Fear that if I ever stopped doing, I'd fall apart. Shadow work isn't about fixing yourself. It's about facing yourself. The Shadow Isn't the Enemy— Avoidance Is. You don't need to kill your shadow. You need to integrate it. Because here's the truth: The Shadow isn't trying to hurt you—it's trying to protect you, based on outdated pain. The angry part of you? It might be defending a younger version of you that was unheard. The insecure part? It might be trying to protect you from humiliation or rejection. The lazy part? It could be burnout wearing a hoodie.

When you stop judging these parts and start getting curious, healing begins. How to Start Doing Shadow Work. You don't need a cave, a retreat, or a therapist (though therapy helps). You need honest reflection, relentless curiosity, and the courage to stop running.

Here's how to begin:

1. Notice Emotional Triggers. What sets you off? Anger, jealousy, defensiveness—those reactions are breadcrumbs to your Shadow.

2. Ask: What Am I Protecting? Go deeper. What part of you feels threatened? What's the real fear behind the reaction?

3. Write Letters You'll Never Send. Let the shadow speak. Write from the part of you that's been ignored or judged. Let it rage, cry, plead. Then read it back with compassion.

4. Use Mirror Work. Look yourself in the eye and say out loud the truths you usually hide. Not affirmations —admissions.

5. Forgive Who You Used to Be. Stop carrying guilt for surviving. That version of you got you this far. Now it's time to evolve.

When You Do the Shadow Work… You stop lashing out. You stop shrinking. You stop proving. You start owning. Owning your past. Owning your flaws. Owning your power. You become whole— not perfect, but integrated. And when a man integrates his shadow? He becomes dangerous in the best way. He can't be manipulated by praise or criticism. He doesn't need the room to love him. He already claimed the parts of himself that used to haunt him. That's real confidence. That's unshakable presence. That's power.

REFLECTION PROMPT:

1. What part of you have you been running from?

2. What would it look like to face that part— not to fight it, but to understand it?

CHAPTER 12.

BUILDING A LIFE THAT FEEDS YOU

Not Just One That Looks Good

Let's get honest: I've built things before that looked amazing from the outside.

- Fit body.
- Hustle grind.
- Business cards.
- Titles.
- Applause.
- Likes.
- "You're killing it, bro."

But I was starving. Because validation doesn't equal fulfillment. Claps don't fill the void. And a life built to look good will eventually feel like a cage.

MOST PEOPLE ARE STARVING IN A LIFE THEY BUILT

Here's the trap: You chase success thinking it will fix you. You get it. Then realize you're still you—with all the same pain, all the same emptiness, just with nicer scenery. This is what happens when you build a life around optics instead of alignment. You're busy, but not grounded. You're impressive, but not at peace. You're successful, but secretly miserable. That's not winning. That's soul-debt. What Actually Feeds You? This is the question most people never ask.

Not:

- "What will get the most attention?"
- "What's the fastest path to money?"
- "What looks successful to others?"

But:

"What actually fills me up when no one's watching?" For me, it wasn't the title. It was meaning. It was knowing I'm getting closer to the man I respect in the mirror. It was helping people—really helping. It was quiet mornings, deep conversations, uncomfortable growth. It was showing up for the life I was called to build, not the one I thought would fix me.

YOU HAVE TO DEFINE "SUCCESS" FOR YOURSELF

If you don't define it, the world will. And the world's definition is loud, shallow, and addicted to speed. You need to build a definition that aligns with your values, not your fears. Success isn't about money, clout, or aesthetics—unless those things actually align with your soul.

Success might be:

- Peace in your nervous system
- Time with your kids
- Mastery of your craft
- Building something slowly but sustainably
- Leaving behind something real, not just flashy

Your life doesn't have to look good to them. It has to feel good to you. How to Start Building a Life That Feeds You

1. **Audit Your Life Honestly**

   Look at each area: work, health, relationships, habits.
   Ask: Does this drain me or feed me? Start subtracting what drains. Start multiplying what feeds.

2. **Unplug From Performance Mode**

   Stop making decisions based on how they'll be perceived. Start making them based on how they'll be experienced.

3. **Find Your Core 3**

    Identify the 3 things that give you energy, clarity, and fire. Protect those with your life.

4. **Stop Comparing Paths**

    You don't need to be ahead of anyone— you just need to be in alignment with your own values. Your timing is sacred. Stay in your lane.

5. **Ask Yourself: "What Will Still Matter at 80?"**

    If it won't matter when you're old and grey, don't let it steal your time now.

BUILD FROM THE INSIDE OUT

The next version of you isn't just about achieving more. It's about becoming more honest, more whole, more you.

A life that feeds you:

- Makes you calm, not just hyped
- Makes you proud, not just praised
- Makes you peaceful, not just productive

Let the others chase trends. You chase truth. That's how you build something that lasts.

REFLECTION PROMPT:

1. What part of your current life is performative?
2. What would change if you stopped trying to impress, and started trying to align?

CHAPTER

13.

THE WORK IS THE WAY

Why the Process Is the Payoff

Let's kill a lie right now: "Once I get there, I'll feel better." That's the trap. The finish line fantasy. The idea that one day you'll arrive, exhale, and everything will make sense. Here's the truth most people avoid:

There is no finish line.

The process is the point.

The work is the reward.

The becoming is the destination.

CHASING THE FEELING WILL BREAK YOU

If you only work when the feeling hits, you'll burn out.

If you only grind for the goal, you'll feel empty when you hit it.

If you only show up for the applause, you'll crumble in silence.

You've got to flip the script:

- Don't train to look good—train to stay dangerous.
- Don't read to impress—read to evolve.
- Don't write to go viral—write to sharpen your voice.
- Don't work to escape—work to engage.
- Don't build to arrive—build to grow.

THE PROCESS IS WHERE YOU BUILD YOUR EDGE

Results are snapshots. The process is the story.

- The grind at 5 a.m.? That's where you build your edge.
- The days you show up with no motivation? That's where you earn your confidence.

- The reps you put in after failure? That's where you find your power. The work is the furnace. The pain is the forge. The process is the proof. Every time you show up, even when it sucks, you reinforce the most powerful belief you can have:

"I'm the kind of person who keeps going." That belief? That's your fuel when everything else runs dry.

Detach From Outcome. Reattach to Discipline

The world tells you to obsess overcoutcomes:

- Followers
- Sales
- Metrics
- Milestones

And yeah, those things matter. But if they're your only metric, you're fragile. Because when the numbers stall, you'll quit. When the likes fade, you'll crumble. When the scale lies, you'll spiral. That's why you have to reattach to the only thing you can fully control: Your discipline. Your ability to show up, do the work, and let the outcome sort itself out.

Fall in Love With the Work—Not the Win Here's the secret:

The people who win long-term? They love the process. They fall in love with the doing, not just the having. They aren't chasing a feeling—they're becoming someone. The "win" is just a byproduct. But the real high? It's in the grind. The craft. The sharpening. This book you're reading?

It wasn't written in a moment of inspiration. It was built word by word—during patrol breaks, late nights, slow days, tired mornings. No crowd. No hype. Just the work. And that's what made it real.

"But It's Not Working Yet…" Yeah. That's the point. It's not supposed to feel good right away. Growth is the result of resistance, not reward. The longer you stay in it without results, the stronger you get. Most people quit in the in-between. They ghost their goals because it "doesn't feel right anymore." But you? You keep showing up. And one day, without even noticing, you'll realize:

"I'm no longer doing the work to get something—I'm doing the work because this is who I am." That's freedom. That's power. That's peace.

REFLECTION PROMPT:

1. If no one ever saw your work— if no one clapped or noticed— would you still do it?

2. What would change if you stopped needing the win and started loving the work?

CHAPTER 14.

BUILDING WHILE BLEEDING

How to Stay in the Game When Life Hits Hard

Let's be honest—this journey doesn't pause when life punches you in the face.

- You still have to show up to work after getting bad news.
- You still have to train when your heart's broken.
- You still have to sell homes, answer emails, raise kids, or walk a beat while your mind is screaming for rest.

This chapter isn't about powering through like a robot. It's about learning how to build while bleeding—to keep going even when your soul feels scraped raw.

PAIN DOESN'T DISQUALIFY YOU—IT DEEPENS YOU

You might think the hard seasons make you less capable. That if you're hurting, struggling, or doubting, you're somehow failing. But here's the truth:

Pain doesn't weaken you. It wakes you up.

- It humbles you.
- It clarifies what really matters.
- It deepens your empathy.
- It sharpens your focus.

Some of the strongest things I've built were born in the middle of heartbreak, confusion, and exhaustion. I didn't wait to feel better. I just kept building—one brick at a time, through the tears, through the noise, through the silence.

YOU'RE ALLOWED TO BLEED—JUST DON'T BOW OUT

This isn't about pretending you're okay.

You can feel the pain.

You can slow down.

You can cry, scream, shake, journal, pray.

But don't disappear. Don't ghost your mission. Don't hand over the pen that writes your story. You can bleed—but don't hand the mic to the part of you that wants to quit.

CREATE A FRAMEWORK FOR THE HARD DAYS

Bad days are coming. Expect them. Prepare for them.

Here's how you stay grounded:

1. Create a Bare Minimum Baseline When life is heavy, simplify.

   - 10 minutes of movement
   - 1 act of service
   - 1 page of reading
   - 1 honest conversation

   That's still progress. That's still you winning.

2. Switch From Performance to Presence. Stop trying to "crush it" every day. Some days, just be there. That's enough.

3. Speak to Yourself Like You Would a Brother. You wouldn't tell a friend who's grieving, "You're weak." You'd say, "You're here. I'm proud of you for not quitting." Say the same to yourself.

4. Honor the Hurt—Then Harness It Use it. Channel it. Turn the ache into action. Write. Train. Build. Express. Not to escape it—but to transform it. The World Needs Your Story —Not Just Your Highlight Reel. Most people hide when they're bleeding.

They Disappear. They isolate. Go dark. Numb out. But what if your greatest strength isn't pretending you're untouchable? What if it's being real? "I'm hurting. And I'm still here." "I'm tired. And I'm still showing up." "I'm doubting. And I'm still moving forward."

That's what inspires people. Not perfection —but perseverance.
You Don't Have to Be Healed to Be Helpful

Don't wait until you've got it all figured out. Your healing can happen as you move. As you help. As you serve. As you build. I've given some of my best advice with tears in my eyes. I've helped people find clarity while I was lost in my own fog. I've shown up for others on days I could barely stand for myself.

And you know what? That mattered. That healed me, too.

ONE BRICK AT A TIME

You're not building a mansion in one day. You're laying bricks. And some bricks will be laid through joy, clarity, and confidence. Others? Through grief, anger, and fear. But they all count. Brick by brick. Breath by breath. Bleeding—but building. That's how you become unstoppable.

REFLECTION PROMPT:

1. What pain are you carrying right now that you've been trying to outrun?

2. What would it look like to bring that pain with you as you move forward, instead of waiting for it to leave?

CHAPTER 15.

THE LONG GAME
How to Win Over Years, Not Just Seasons

Everyone's chasing quick.

Quick results.

Quick money.

Quick validation.

Quick growth.

And it's killing their depth. It's killing their roots. It's killing their power. We live in a world that treats patience like weakness and consistency like boredom. But here's the truth no one wants to hear: Most of the people you admire didn't get there fast. They just didn't quit.

Microwave Success Is a Lie. You see someone blow up on social media, and it looks like they made it overnight.

What you don't see:

- The years of grinding when no one was watching
- The failed attempts before the breakthrough
- The doubt, the setbacks, the restarts
- The nights they wanted to quit but kept going anyway

Fast success is usually fake. And real success is usually slow. You Have to Decide: Are You Here to Impress or Endure?

If you're chasing fast results, you'll quit the moment it gets hard. But if you're committed to the long game, you'll keep showing up—even when it's slow, quiet, and thankless. Anyone can grind for a week. Anyone can be consistent when they're inspired. But can you stay locked in:

- When the likes disappear?
- When the money's low?

- When no one's watching?
- When you feel like you're falling behind? That's the test. That's what separates the real ones from the posers.

PLAY LONG ENOUGH, AND YOU CAN'T LOSE

Here's the cheat code most people ignore: If you keep showing up, you eventually win.

It's math. It's physics. It's life. The compound effect is real:

- Small actions, done consistently, over time, create unstoppable momentum.
- One rep doesn't change your body—but a thousand will.
- One cold call doesn't build your business —but hundreds will.
- One deep conversation doesn't fix your relationships—but many do. Stay in the game long enough, and your current self won't recognize your future self.

You Need a 10-Year Mindset Not 10 minutes. Not 10 weeks. 10 years.

Ask yourself:

"What would happen if I stayed consistent for the next decade?" "What if I stopped quitting every time I got bored, tired, or discouraged?" 10 years of:

- Training
- Studying
- Creating
- Healing
- Practicing
- Rebuilding
- Serving

- Learning
- Growing

That's legacy. That's power. That's peace.

YOU DON'T NEED TO BLOW UP— YOU NEED TO GROW DEEP

Big isn't the goal. Rooted is. The oak tree doesn't rush. It grows slow and steady. Storms come and go—but it stays. Why? Because its roots are deep. Be like that. Let others chase trends. Let them burn out. You? You grow deep. Consistency Is a Superpower Not motivation. Not intensity. Consistency. That boring, unsexy, relentless repetition of the basics.

That's what builds:

- Mastery
- Resilience
- Peace
- Reputation
- Freedom

You're not falling behind—you're compounding.

You're not slow—you're strategic. You're not forgotten—you're becoming.

REFLECTION PROMPT:

1. If you fully committed to the long game for the next 5–10 years, what would your life look like?
2. What habits are you planting now that your future self will thank you for?

CHAPTER 16.

THE DISCIPLINE SHIFT
From Wanting to Willing

You want it. I know you do.

- You want peace.
- You want confidence.
- You want freedom, impact, clarity, direction.
- You want to feel like you're becoming the version of you that doesn't flinch anymore. But wanting isn't enough.

Everybody wants. Everybody dreams. Everybody talks about who they could be if only… Wanting is cheap. Willingness?

That's rare. Discipline Isn't Rigid—It's Freedom. Most people treat discipline like a punishment.

They think:

- "If I get disciplined, I'll be less happy."
- "I'll have less freedom."
- "I won't enjoy life."

But the truth is the opposite. Discipline creates the life you actually want.

Discipline means:

- Freedom from regret
- Freedom from chaos
- Freedom from addiction to moods
- Freedom to be proud of who you are— even when no one's looking

The people with the most freedom in their lives are almost always the most disciplined.

WILLINGNESS > MOTIVATION

You will not always be motivated. You will not always feel like showing up. But you can always be willing.

Willingness means:

- Showing up tired
- Showing up unsure
- Showing up afraid
- Showing up when it's boring
- Showing up when no one claps

Willingness says:

"This matters more than my comfort right now."

Discipline Isn't Glamorous—It's Gritty. No music. No spotlight. No adrenaline rush. Just the same actions, again and again, stacked brick by brick in the dark. You want to change your life?

- Wake up and move your body when it's the last thing you want to do.
- Say no to distractions when no one's watching.
- Be kind when you're angry.
- Be honest when it's easier to lie.
- Do the reps. Do the reading. Do the journaling. Do the work. Not once. Not for a week. Relentlessly. Because this is who you are now.

You Don't Need a New Plan—You Need a New Standard Most people don't fail from lack of knowledge. They fail because they tolerate too much slack. You want better results? Raise the standard. Don't wait for a new opportunity, new job, new relationship, new spark. Show up like the person who's already there.

Stop wanting. Start willing. That's the shift. The Man You're Becoming Is Already in You He's not "out there." He's not waiting on a perfect time, perfect plan, or perfect mood. He's in you now. Right here. Right under the fear, the doubt, the stories, the noise. You don't find him. You build him. With every disciplined choice. Every uncomfortable conversation. Every rep, every journal entry, every early alarm. Every time you say, "I don't feel like it, but I'm doing it anyway." You're Not Done—You're Just Getting Started

This isn't a story about "making it." This is a story about making you. I'm still in it. Still working patrol. Still running my real estate business. Still grinding in the dark with no guarantee. Still dragging my shadows into the light. Still learning to love the process. And so are you. So don't stop. Don't overthink. Don't quit because it's hard. Double down because it's hard. You're not lost—you're in the forge. You're not behind —you're building slow roots. You're not broken—you're becoming unbreakable.

FINAL REFLECTION:

1. What would change if you stopped asking, "What do I want?" And started asking, "What am I willing to do —every day—to become the person I said I would be?"

2. This Is the Path It's not clean. It's not glamorous. It's not linear. But it's real. And it's yours. If you're reading this and you're still in the dark— good. You're not alone. I'm here with you. We're building something that can't be shaken. Let the world chase shortcuts. You?

3. You show up. You suffer well. You build while bleeding. You play the long game. You become unrecognizable. You become unstoppable.

AUTHOR'S NOTE ON CONCEPTS REFERENCED

Some ideas explored in this book—such as Carl Jung's Shadow, the Law of Diminishing Intent, and the Law of Equivalent Exchange—are drawn from well-known psychological or philosophical frameworks. While not quoted directly, they have influenced my thinking and approach to personal growth. I encourage readers to explore these deeper for themselves.

BLURB:

This isn't a fairy tale. It's not a highlight reel This is a war journal from the middle of the grind. I wasn't born for greatness. I was the overweight kid in special ed. The one with labels, doubt, and something to prove. I chased validation through fitness, money, careers, and titles—trainer, agent, cop. None of it filled the void.

Until I stopped chasing motivation… and started building discipline. This book is for anyone who's tired of starting over. For anyone stuck in the suck, wondering if it's even worth it. It's not about "making it." It's about still showing up— especially when no one's watching.

If you're waiting for motivation, you're already behind. If you're in the dark right now—good. That's where transformation begins.

🔥 The Realest Self-Help Book You'll Ever Read

🛠 Written in the grind. Not after it.

📱 Instagram: @fckmotiv

✉ fckmotiv@gmail.comy

Forget Motivation

www.ingramcontent.com/pod-product-compliance
Lightning Source LLC
Chambersburg PA
CBHW050612100526
44584CB00038B/3110